The Persian Gulf:
After Iran's Revolution

by J. C. Hurewitz

CONTENTS

HEADLINE Series 244, April 1979   **$1.40**

Cover design: Cathy Canzani

The Author

J. C. HUREWITZ is professor of government and
director of the Middle East Institute of Columbia
University. He is advisory editor of the *Middle
East Journal* and a member of the boards of
governors of the Middle East Institute and the
American Research Center in Egypt, and was a
founder and the first vice-president of the American Institute on Iranian Studies. He has lived and
traveled widely in the Middle East and is the
author of many books, including *Middle East
Politics: The Military Dimension.* Volume 2 of his
three-volume work, *The Middle East and North
Africa in World Politics,* has just been published.

The Foreign Policy Association

The Foreign Policy Association is a private, nonprofit, nonpartisan educational
organization. Its purpose is to stimulate wider interest and more effective
participation in, and greater understanding of, world affairs among American
citizens. Among its activities is the continuous publication, dating from 1935, of
the HEADLINE Series pamphlets. The authors of these pamphlets are responsible for factual accuracy and for the views expressed. FPA itself takes no position
on issues of United States foreign policy.

The HEADLINE Series (ISSN 0017-8780) is published February, April, August,
October and December by the Foreign Policy Association, Inc., 345 East 46th St.,
New York, N.Y. 10017. Chairman, Carter L. Burgess; Editor, Wallace Irwin, Jr.;
Associate Editor, Gwen Crowe. Subscription rates, $7.00 for 5 issues; $13.00 for 10
issues; $18.00 for 15 issues. Single copy price $1.40. Discount 25% on 10 to 99 copies;
30% on 100 to 499; 35% on 500 to 999; 40% on 1,000 or more. Payment must
accompany order for $5 or less. Second-class postage paid at New York, N.Y.
Copyright 1979 by Foreign Policy Association, Inc. Composed and printed at
Science Press, Ephrata, Penn.

Library of Congress Catalog No. 790312
ISBN 0-87124-054-8

1

Renewed Need for Stability

Five years ago, in the wake of the October 1973 Arab-Israeli war
and the international oil crisis that accompanied it, I addressed
in a study for the HEADLINE Series the question of political stability
in the Persian Gulf, and the role of the United States in promoting
that goal. The question had arisen primarily from the departure of
Britain in 1971 after a century and a half of political paramountcy
in the Gulf. Two years later, the question had taken on greater
importance than ever because of the sudden growth in the wealth
and consequent international influence or "oil power" of the states

Editor's note: *Many readers will recall the author's essay "The
Persian Gulf: Prospects for Stability"* (HEADLINE Series *220, April
1974). The upheaval in Iran in 1978–79 has created new conditions
and raised new questions about U.S. interests and policies in the
region. Since these questions can be understood only in the context of
political, diplomatic, economic and social affairs in the Gulf and
nearby areas, we asked Dr. Hurewitz to update his 1974 study and its
statistical tables and write new chapters on recent developments and
their implications for the United States.*

of the region. Whether the desired stability was achievable, and how the United States would go about promoting it, could not then be clearly foreseen.

Again today, a second crisis, the revolution in Iran, has jarred American opinion into a new phase of attention to the affairs of the Gulf. At the time of writing, that upheaval had not yet run its course, and where it might end no one could safely predict. But it had already started shock waves that were felt across the world. The deposition of the shah, America's chief *de facto* ally in the region, sent shudders through the extended royal family of America's other principal friend in the Gulf, Saudi Arabia. It alarmed the quasi monarchies that rule the ministates on the Arabian shore of the Gulf and even the Socialist regime in Iraq. It was altering the balance of power in the Middle East and adding fresh uncertainties to the Arab-Israeli dispute, whose protean shape changed once again in March 1979 with the signing of the peace treaty between Israel and Egypt. It was causing widespread cancellation of contracts for sale to Iran of armaments and many other items made in the industrial West, and a massive outflow of Western nationals, how permanently none could say.

And on the energy front, it was disorienting the international energy industries, inducing the industrial states to curtail oil consumption, making nuclear energy with all its hazards once more a front-page issue, reducing by nearly half the daily consumption of natural gas in the Soviet Caucasus, enabling the Organization of Petroleum Exporting Countries (OPEC) to raise yet again the price of crude oil—thereby further enlarging the negative payments balance of the United States and further depressing the value of the dollar.

Most pertinent to our present study, the events in Iran were unraveling among the Persian Gulf states themselves the seven-year-old, largely self-regulating interstate system that had superseded the age of British hegemony. Thus new targets of opportunity opened for Arab radicalism and for possible Soviet political manipulation.

No American government could remain unconcerned over these events, for they affect, actually or potentially, major and enduring U.S. interests. First and most obvious among these interests is oil. The Persian Gulf will remain for some years to come, for better or worse, a major source of energy supplies for the United States and, even more, for our European and Japanese allies—on terms which have been set since 1973 primarily by the decisions, often politically influenced, of the oil-exporting countries themselves. Second, effective relations must be maintained with the Arab states of the Gulf because of their major weight in the Arab confrontation with Israel. (How long the shah's successors in Iran may continue their proclaimed Islamic solidarity with the anti-Israeli cause will depend largely on their ability to establish a durable Islamic republic.) Finally, connected with these major interests is a third: to

Charismatic leader of the Iranian revolution that, the author says, "started shock waves that were felt across the world": Ayatallah Ruhallah Khomeini receives an ecstatic welcome in Tehran after return February 1, 1979, from 14-year exile.

Wide World Photos

prevent the Soviet Union, Iran's next-door neighbor, from projecting its influence at American expense into the Gulf, the Arabian peninsula, and the nearby shores of the Indian Ocean and the Red Sea.

In the wake of the Iranian upheaval, two kinds of threat to American interests seemed to arise. One fear was that the political-religious Islamic fundamentalism that has been called "Khomeini fever" might prove contagious, spreading from Iran through Saudi Arabia and Oman and the sheikhdoms of the Gulf. The other fear was that left-wing political movements would continue to ally themselves with Soviet power in the region, as they had recently done in the People's Democratic Republic of Yemen (PDRY), the nearby Horn of Africa and Afghanistan. These trends, in turn, could polarize still further the Israeli-Arab conflict and endanger the tenuous new accord between Israel and Egypt. Such fears were by no means confined to Washington. Indeed, it was above all the rulers of the patriarchal oil-producing states of the Gulf who noted that the United States, which had saved the shah's throne a quarter-century earlier, appeared powerless to do so again; and they began to wonder about the future value to them of the American connection.

In the circumstances of early 1979, stability became the watchword of the Carter Administration's improvised policy on the Gulf, and renewal of stability became the supreme object of a wide-ranging diplomacy. Clearly, the achievement of this aim would first require rebuilding the trust of friendly Arab leaders in the readiness of the United States to shore up their position with effective political, diplomatic and military props.

It seems possible as this is written that the U.S. response may be more direct than it was in 1972 after Britain's departure from the Gulf. At that time, with the war in Vietnam still far from over, neither the Congress nor the public would countenance new American commitments abroad; hence, whatever new regional system replaced that of Britain had to be at least ostensibly self-regulating. Seven years later, these inhibitions on American policy seem to have diminished, and the prospect arises that the United States may emerge as a more visible balancer of power in the region.

6

2

The Gulf and U.S. Interests

For well over a century, British India, and later Britain itself, served as the political stabilizer in the Persian Gulf at three levels—domestic, regional and international. Starting in 1820, the British presence grew step by step: from suppressor of piracy and slave trading, to truce supervisor, to manager of external sovereignty and inescapable meddler in internal affairs, to precluder of other European concession- and base-seekers, to explicit precluder of oil-concession seekers—all in the name of defender of India. When Britain gave India independence in 1947, it persisted in its privileged role in the Gulf as protector of the sources of oil supply and later invited the United States to establish a token naval presence as reinforcer of the credibility of Britain's "exclusive" presence.

Early in 1968, when Britain gave four years' notice of its intention to leave the Gulf, almost every close observer expected the worst, some predicting regional anarchy. The anxiety mounted because of the high dependence of Western Europe and Japan and the anticipated growing dependence of the United States on Persian Gulf oil.

Oil Resources

More than three-fifths of the world's proved crude oil reserves are located in the states that rim the Persian Gulf and lie beneath its bed. Close to 57 percent of Western Europe's oil in 1971 came from the Gulf; the comparable figure for Japan approached 90 percent. In the 1970s, U.S. imports from the Gulf began to rise and now account for one-seventh of all U.S. oil consumption. (See table, page 57.) According to a 1972 assessment of the National Petroleum Council, the industry's advisory body to the U.S. Department of the Interior:

> A secure domestic energy base is a vital element of national security; overdependence on foreign sources can make the United States vulnerable to interruption of petroleum supply from military action or from shutdown for political reasons. Without the deterrent effect of a strong domestic oil industry, producing countries could more easily threaten economic sanctions and boycotts to significantly influence U.S. international policies. Moreover, major supply interruptions of energy imports could severely hamper the functioning of the U.S. economy.

This study will not analyze the role of the Gulf and its bordering states in the oil—and energy—crisis as such. But the political side effects in the Gulf of that crisis and the continuing political interplay between the Gulf and the major oil-importing states cannot be ignored. Ever since 1945, U.S. security planners have subscribed to the doctrine that this country must not rely on oil supplies outside the Western Hemisphere. In the 1970s, with U.S. oil consumption steadily outrunning domestic production, this doctrine ceased to be workable. Well into the 1980s and in all likelihood beyond, the United States and its allies will probably have little choice but to look to the Persian Gulf for crude oil to slake their growing energy thirst. This is the price they have to pay for the failure to develop comprehensive energy policies that take adequately into account the unfolding realities. The lessening of this dependence—a goal sought, thus far without success, by every President since the crisis of 1973—may help in part to reduce the tendency of the Gulf oil states and of the other members of OPEC never to lose an opportunity of a related political crisis to raise the price of crude oil. For full effect, however, the United States and the other industrial importing states will have to relearn the art of political cooperation and organization in dealing with the organized oil-exporting states. Whether the shock of Iran's cutoff of oil exports in 1978–79 sufficed to infuse new vigor into the feeble four-year-old International Energy Agency could not yet be known as this was written.

One further preliminary note is essential. The United States inherited from the United Kingdom the "responsibility" for containing the U.S.S.R. and its projected influence: (1) on the Continent, in Central Europe; (2) in the Mediterranean, at the Turkish straits; (3) in the Far East, on the borders of China; and (4) east of Suez, in the Persian Gulf. Crises of transferral involving the first three of these areas occurred at a time of self-confidence, when the people and government of the United States, convinced of the moral rectitude of their views and policies, were determined to resist by all means the spread of international communism. The fourth transferral crisis broke at a moment of limited *détente* with the U.S.S.R. and Communist China and of self-doubt, which transmuted decisiveness into ambivalence.

Since 1945 the Soviet Union has never sought détente except from a position of parity. This has been true in every limited postwar negotiation between the superpowers including the test-ban treaty, the nonproliferation treaty, SALT I, Helsinki, and, most recently, SALT II. In the Gulf, narrowly conceived, there is no present or early prospect of parity except on terms unacceptable to the United States and the West. This suggests that we are probably destined to live with the regional and international instability that prevails in and near the Gulf, and the best that we might reasonably hope for is the discovery of some mode of balancing that instability. It is still premature at the time of writing to assess the long-range effects of the major parallel events of 1978–79 in the Middle East—the Iranian revolution and the Israeli-Egyptian treaty—on the emerging balance in the Gulf. But the need for a balance is undeniable, and its achievement is bound to depend heavily on the United States.

3

The Riparians: Majors and Ministates

In their relative magnitudes, the eight states in the Gulf fall into three classes (table, p. 12; map, p. 32): one superstate, Iran, with a population of more than 35 million; two majors, Iraq (12.5 million) and Saudi Arabia (about 5.5 million); and the ministates with populations of 1 million or less. Of approximately 57 million people living in the Gulf states, 94 percent are bunched in three countries—Iran, Iraq and Saudi Arabia. Five-eighths of the overall total are Iranians. Saudi Arabia has never taken a census, and the figure of 5.5 million is no more than an informed "guesstimate." The five ministates have a probable combined population of fewer than 3.5 million, of whom at least one-third are recent settlers. Technicians, unskilled workers and adventurers, they have been lured by the fantastic prosperity, chiefly of Kuwait, Qatar and Abu Dhabi. The immigrants and long-term residents—the majority, Palestinians and expatriates from the Arab states, and the rest, Pakistanis, Indians and Iranians—are denied citizenship and the privileges that go with it. Yet they continue coming, in search of the well-paid jobs and the opportunities for making fortunes.

All the Gulf states, large and small, are oil producers. In 1977 Saudi Arabia, Iran and Iraq exported 72 percent of the total, and if

Kuwait and the United Arab Emirates are added, 88 percent of the total. In 1977 these exports brought returns exceeding $91 billion, or more than a tenfold increase in five years.

In economic and social terms, the Gulf is a region of rapid change; but political change, as might be expected, lags behind. As recently as 1945, all the Gulf states had substantial tribal populations and no other section of the Middle East could claim to be more traditional. After a generation of rapid expansion of the oil industry, some of the Gulf states rank among the most modern in the Middle East. But—despite growing educational and other contact with the democratic West—none is democratic. Much as we may prefer to support liberal political systems, these are not likely to appear among the Gulf states in the coming decade. Leaving aside for the moment the still unsettled question of Iran, all the polities are authoritarian, and all those in the Arabian peninsula are monarchical or quasi monarchical. When Soviet propaganda labels a government "progressive," as it has the military government of Iraq, read it as meaning "friendly to the U.S.S.R."

Long before the fall of the shah, U.S. and Western European observers were exercised over problems of succession in the Gulf. Under the British system, the United Kingdom had guaranteed the "dynastic" lines in the ministates, on good behavior. The rare change was invariably intradynastic and always managed with stability in mind. With the controls lifted on the British departure, the results were bound to be unstabilizing—or so, at least, many Westerners thought. They noted how Iraq under the monarchy had been a staunch ally of the West in the unfolding postwar regional crises, but with the coming of the soldier rulers in 1958 had turned increasingly to the U.S.S.R. for assistance. According to the prevailing fear in the West, military *coups d'état* are likely to spread in the Gulf, since it is commonly held by political scientists that monarchies are on the way out. We will come back to this question in a later chapter.

The Superstate—Iran

Iran is the most populous of the riparian states. Its 35 million people show wide ethnic and linguistic diversity. Those who speak Farsi (Persian) as their mother tongue, while forming the largest community, constitute at best only a slight majority. The Kurds and

	Area (thousand sq. mi.)	Population[1] (thousands)		Oil Reserve (billion barre	
		1972	1978	1972	197
SUPERSTATE:					
Iran	628.0	30,805	35,400	65.0	62
MAJOR STATES:					
Iraq	170.0	10,142	12,470	29	34
Saudi Arabia	830.0	4,000	5,500	146[3]	153
MINISTATES:					
Bahrain	0.32	233	345	0.4	0
Kuwait	8.0	957	1,160	73[3]	70
Oman	82.0	678	837	5.0	5
Qatar	8.5	89	205	7.0	5
United Arab Emirates:	36.0	178.6	875	23.0	32
Abu Dhabi	32.0	46		21.0	31
Dubai	1.5	59		2.0	1
al-Sharjah	1.0	31.5			0
Ajman	0.1	4.2			
Umm al-Qaiwain	0.3	3.7			
Ras al-Khaimah	0.65	24.5			
al-Fujairah	0.65	24.5			
			Total:	371.38	396
			World Total:	666.88	645

[1]Estimates.

[2]Estimated proved reserves from "Worldwide Report," *Oil and Gas Journal*, 25 December 1972 a December 1977.

[3]Including half share of Neutral Zone.

[4]OPEC, *Annual Statistical Bulletin*, 1977.

[5]*Petroleum Economist*, July 1978, pp. 285–286. The figures for Bahrain and Oman are derived fro International Monetary Fund, *International Financial Statistics*, vol. 32 (March 1979). The fiscal year of from 21 March–20 March. The fiscal year of Kuwait was changed in 1975–1976 from 1 April–31 Marc July–30 June.

[6]IISS, *The Military Balance, 1972–1973, 1973–1974, 1978–1979*. For the four principal countri breakdown by armed services is as follows:

	Oil Production[4] (thousand barrels)		Oil Revenue[5] ($ billion)		GNP[6] ($ billion)		Armed Forces[6] (thousands)		Defense Budget[6] ($ million)	
	1972	1977	1972	1977	1972	1977	1972	1978	1972	1978
	023.1	5,662.8	2.4	23.0	15.1	72.6	210.5[6]	413.0[6]	2,010	9,940
	465.5	2,493.0	0.57	9.6	3.5	16.3	102.0[6]	212.0[6]	338	1,660
	016.3[3]	9,200.0[3]	3.1[3]	37.8[3]	5.2	55.4	42.0[6]	58.5[6]	1,090	9,630
	69.7	58.2	0.1	0.5	0.28	1.7	1.1	2.3	3.5	43.0
	283.0[3]	1,969.0[3]	1.7[3]	8.5[3]	3.7	12.0	1.1[6]	12.0[6]	98.9	322.2
	281.8	343.2	0.2	1.6	0.21	2.5	9.2	19.2	50.0	767.0
	482.4	444.6	0.25	1.9	0.53	2.4	1.8	4.0		61.0
	202.7	1,998.7	0.55	8.3		7.7	10.0[7]	25.9	114.0	661.0
							6.0			
							1.0			
							0.25			
							0.25			
							0.21			
	71.5	24,199.5	8.87	91.2						
	885.6	60,210.8								

	Army		Air Force		Navy	
	1972	1978	1972	1978	1972	1978
	160,000	285,000	22,000	100,000	9,000	28,000
i Arabia	90,000	180,000	9,800	28,000	2,000	4,000
ait	36,000	45,000	3,500	12,000	1,000	1,500
	7,000	10,500	2,000	1,000	200	500

rall number in the United Arab Emirates; the Union Defense Force, as such, consisted of only 1,600.

Baluchis, who speak languages related to Persian, are Sunnis or orthodox Muslims, as are also the Arabs of Khuzistan, the major oil-producing province. These linguistic, ethnic and sectarian minorities have traditionally resisted centralized rule, in which the late Pahlavi dynasty compelled them at sword's point to acquiesce.

Iran has the longest coastline on the Gulf (more than 600 miles) and, under the monarchy, had a military establishment larger and more modern than all the rest combined. For 25 years after his American-backed return to Iran, following the overthrow of the Mosaddegh government in 1953, Mohammad Reza Shah Pahlavi, the country's ruler, proved hardier than most observers predicted. After outlasting several major internal political crises, in the third decade of his rule, the shah launched a program of economic and social development unprecedented in his kingdom; he employed the steadily multiplying oil revenues to finance the expansion, which in turn yielded many new sources of income. The shahdom's gross national product (GNP) rose between 1960 and 1970 from $3.9 billion to $10.8 billion, climbing to $15.1 billion in 1972 and rocketing to $72.6 billion five years later. Still, Iran remained a police state, and the shah, while retaining exclusive policy-making powers, entrusted the management of his realm to technocrats, carefully chosen for loyalty as well as ability—a common pattern among the authoritarian polities that abound in the Middle East.

As we shall note in a later chapter, the revolution of 1978 revealed many weaknesses that proved fatal to the shah's rule.

Saudi Arabia

Saudi Arabia has far the greatest proved oil reserves of any state in the Gulf, indeed in the world, and is the world's leading oil exporter—a position reached after four decades of oil development primarily by a U.S. concessionary consortium. Yet despite its great oil wealth, it makes no sense to compare development in Saudi Arabia with that in Iran because the Saudi population is so small and is distributed unevenly over a vast, largely desert kingdom. The Saudi dynasty, by retaining in its hands the key ministries such as defense, the national guard and the interior, has successfully resisted radicalization. Even before the assassination of King Faisal in 1975, apprehension grew over what many felt would become a

King Abdul-Aziz ibn
Saud, founder of the
dynasty that rules
Saudi Arabia

succession crisis after his death. But, as those more familiar with the
Saudi system predicted, the problem of succession in Saudi Arabia
proved far less acute than in Iran. A precedent had been established
in 1964 when a majority of the sons of the founder of the kingdom,
Abdul-Aziz ibn Saud (reigned 1902–53), in clannish council forced
the abdication of King Saud (1953–64) for incompetence and named
Faisal the successor. In the absence of primogeniture, understand-
able tensions and rivalries arise among eligible brothers. So far,
these have been held in check by the practice of designating a crown
prince as the next in line at the time of the accession of a new king.
For uncontested succession, clannish cohesion is essential—and it
has worked.

Such cohesion is indeed traditional in Islam. The great 14th-
century historical sociologist, Abdul Rahman ibn Khaldun, found a
word for it—*asabiyyah,* the feeling of solidarity or cohesion within a
tribe—on which he based his famous theory of Arab dynastic cycles.
This tradition was reinforced by the foresight of the founder of the
Saudi Arab state, who was literally the father of the kingdom. By
rotating his marriages to the daughters of the leading tribal chiefs of
the Nejd as he assimilated their districts into his expanding state,
Ibn Saud fashioned an assembly line for the production of princes
and for the conversion of a family into a clan. He left more than 30
living sons from the many unions. This was not merely procreation-

al. It was creative kingdom-building. It provided a large pool of candidates for succession. More important, it knitted the sprawling, sparsely populated Nejdi desert into a cohering district. There is hardly an influential tribe in the Nejd that is not directly or indirectly related to the royal clan, thus giving each a vested interest in the continuance of the present system.

This is not to suggest that the problems of succession in Saudi Arabia have disappeared. On the contrary, as living standards steadily rise, and more and more villagers and tribesmen as well as the urban poor receive education and widen their horizons, they may be expected to demand opportunities for political participation. But so long as the economy is expanding and the country is enjoying uninterrupted prosperity, such political discontent may well be moderated before it hardens into organized political opposition.

Iraq

Ever since the overturn of the monarchy in 1958, Iraq has labeled itself a republic, but it is a military republic. In a polity governed by soldiers, there is rarely a formal mode of succession. Instead, leaders are changed by recurrent military coups d'état, and each military junta or despot is always subject to possible overturn by rival officers. The problem has been compounded by the seemingly immutable principle that only the Sunni Arab officers are eligible candidates for the top military and political posts. The Sunni Arab officers, however, come from a minority community within Iraq. Though, like Sunni Arabs elsewhere, the military rulers of Iraq seek to align themselves with the Arab unity movement, they are nonetheless compelled to restrain such inclinations because of the opposition of the Kurds and, to some degree also, of the country's majority, the Shi'ite Arabs.

With four changes of regime in its first decade, republican Iraq hardly experienced continuity of leadership or policy. Instead, each successive regime, whether "collegial" or personal, soon developed as its overriding purpose not public service, but self-service. Yet Iraq paraded itself in the Arab world as the upholder of virtue, the promoter of Arab nationalism and the preserver of Arabism in the Gulf. On the whole, these military governments in Iraq made a mess of their opportunities, and must have caused no little anxiety to their Soviet patrons. The rising returns from oil in the 1960s were mostly dissipated in an inconclusive, useless civil war with the Kurds in the north.

The present Ba'athi regime, the longest-lived of Iraq's postwar military political systems, came into being in July 1968. Its major achievement was the termination in 1975 of the 15-year-old civil war with the Kurds. This was accomplished in a package deal with Iran, which settled a complex boundary dispute that had plagued the relations between the two states ever since the overturn of the monarchy in Iraq. By 1979 the revolution in Iran seemed likely to stir the border-straddling Kurds into new rebellion, this time against both governments.

The Ministates

A source of concern for the Western powers, since the British political withdrawal from the Gulf, has been the questionable viability of all but one of the oil-rich Arab ministates along the Gulf. The one exception is the Emirate (sheikhdom) of Kuwait, which

Lifeblood of the energy-hungry industrial world flows out of the Persian Gulf in vessels like this 200,000-ton British supertanker, taking on a cargo of crude oil in Kuwait.

Wide World Photos

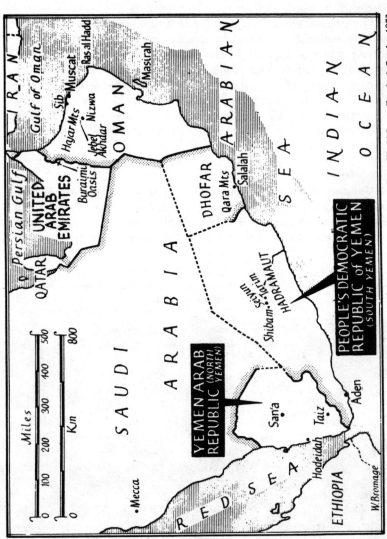

From *World Survey* (London), October 1973

has served for the ministates as a model for rapid economic development and paternalistic welfare statehood. But even Kuwait's experiment with representative institutions ran into trouble. An elected national assembly of 50 deputies, which came into being in 1963 to share the legislative power with the emir, was suspended 13 years later. On the other hand, the ruling Sabah clan has surrendered some of the seats in the cabinet to other Kuwaiti politicians.

Of the remaining ministates, the most developed economically and socially is Bahrain. For a time around 1970 it appeared that Bahrain, then the most populous of the group, might take the lead in a new federation of nine tiny sheikhdoms which Britain contrived to assemble along the Arabian coast of the Gulf. But Bahrain's much-diminished oil revenues could not compete with those of Abu Dhabi, whose Sheikh Zayed bin Sultan al Nahyan became the leader of the new United Arab Emirates (UAE) when it came into being in 1971. Bahrain, as did Qatar, thereupon went its separate way to sovereignty and United Nations membership.

The seven sheikhdoms, the erstwhile Trucial States, that joined to form the UAE (see inset map, page 33) were the most vulnerable candidates for violent succession. With populations ranging from 60,000 down to less than 4,000, they could hardly have been expected to stand on their own. Only three are oil producers: Abu Dhabi, Dubai and, on a marginal scale, al-Sharjah. Britain's purpose in fostering the UAE was to prevent political anarchy in the group, and thus far the purpose has been achieved.

Next to Abu Dhabi, the most significant element in the UAE, is the commercially-minded sheikhdom of Dubai. Even in the pre-oil era, Dubai had learned how to turn an honest penny from its brisk trade as the Gulf's market for industrial imports—including luxury goods often proscribed in Iran and the subcontinent, its main reexport markets—and from smuggling gold to these countries. On becoming an oil-producer in 1969, Dubai added substantially to its income.

When Sheikh Zayed was elected UAE president, Sheikh Rashid of Dubai became vice-president, and both were reelected for further five-year terms. The Federal Supreme Council, comprising the seven rulers, is the policy-making organ on matters within the union's jurisdiction.

Proof of the viability of the UAE, and of the emirate of Qatar as well, soon came when each survived its first succession crisis. Under the veiled-protectorate system, Britain had assured the preservation of the sheikhly dynastic lines. Occasionally when a sheikh failed to cooperate with Britain, he was replaced by a more pliant relative, as had occurred in Sharjah in 1965, when Khalid was installed in his cousin Saqr's place. Less than two months after Britain surrendered sovereignty to the UAE, Saqr with a handful of rebels seized and killed Khalid and a number of his intimate advisers before he himself was forced to give up. Again in Qatar in 1972, another sheikh, Khalifah, seized power from his cousin Ahmed, absent at the time on a hunting trip in Iran. Such forcible "clannish revolutions" are a time-honored mode of changing rulers in the large as well as the tribal Islamic monarchies. The significant fact is that the post-1971 instances of this familiar pattern did not upset the new order.

Finally, the largest in area of all the minuscule principalities, Oman, qualifies as a Gulf state because it lines the western shore of the entrance to the Gulf, and the inner tip of its Musandam peninsula actually falls within the Gulf. It was known as Muscat and Oman until July 1970, when Sultan Qabus bin Said forcibly replaced his father.

4

From Pax Britannica to
Balanced Instability

With the emergence of the ministates described in the preceding chapter, Britain ended a political overlordship in the Persian Gulf that had lasted a century and a half. The British system had its origins in the treaty of 1820, which the government of British-ruled India compelled the sheikh of Bahrain and the sheikhs of the Arabian coast east of Qatar to sign. The treaty, designed to eliminate piracy and the slave trade, did not outlaw war, so that piracy under the name of tribal warfare at sea, especially in the pearl-fishing season, continued to thrive. To stop the practice altogether, the government of India forced the sheikhs in 1835 to accept a six-month truce with the clear understanding that it would apply to fighting at sea but not on land. Periodically renewed until 1843, the truce was extended for ten years and then made permanent—whence the label of Trucial Coast that is still attached to that section of the Gulf's littoral. For the suppression of piracy and later for truce supervision, British India deployed a naval squadron in the Gulf.

The 'Special Treaty' System

Between 1880 and 1916, the government of British India concluded with each sheikh a "special treaty" under which the ruler surrendered external sovereignty to the United Kingdom and pledged not to "cede, sell, mortgage or otherwise give for occupation" any part of his land except to the British government. Between 1913 and 1922 the bonds were reinforced by explicit undertakings not to issue oil concessions without prior British endorsement. Starting with the signature of the treaty of 1820, British India regularly assigned an official from its political service to reside at Bushire on the Persian coast to oversee British interests in the Gulf. In Persia this official held the title of consul general, and as such was a functionary of the British Foreign Office. On the Arabian coast he was known as "political resident," responsible to the government of India and the India Office, and assisted by British political officers and political agents. Jurisdiction over these arrangements passed to the British Foreign Office on the independence of India in 1947.

Britain's main purpose in the Gulf after 1880 was to defend India against possible European encroachment. The earlier interest in trade had become secondary. As Lord Lansdowne, the foreign secretary, said in 1903 in his classic statement of policy on the Persian Gulf, the United Kingdom would "regard the establishment of a naval base, or of a fortified port, in the Persian Gulf by any other power as a very grave menace to British interests," an act which would be resisted "with all the means at our disposal." Commerce without concessions could be no more than minimal, and in the interwar years the United Kingdom did not sanction American oil concessions in the British preserve without a struggle. Until Britain's rule in India ended, its military exclusiveness in the Gulf was complete, being marginally modified only in 1949 to admit the continuous presence of a token American Middle East Force. Britain did not permit even the riparian powers to erect military facilities on the coast or to maintain naval vessels in the Gulf.

End of the Pax Britannica

Before the discovery of oil in the Gulf, the *Pax Britannica* along the Arabian coast had a political rather than an economic purpose:

to shut other European powers out by establishing preclusive protectorates. There was no revenue in the pre-oil age for experiments in planned economic and social change. In any case, the government of India before 1914 would not, in all likelihood, have entertained them. As a result, the governing structures of the veiled protectorates were substantially frozen in their original condition, with little or no innovation.

The discovery of oil in the 1930s changed the situation. It became possible for the producing minidependencies—Bahrain, Kuwait, Qatar and Abu Dhabi, in that order—to launch self-sustaining development programs. (Actually, the sheikh of Bahrain had begun to introduce political and social reforms into his emirate even before crude exports assured him a steady income.) The oil-rich tribalities, once the funds flowed in, were transformed overnight, while their oil-poor neighbors remained largely unaffected. Meanwhile, after 1947, by deliberate choice Western European, and a decade later Japanese, reliance on Persian Gulf oil mounted steadily.

As the Gulf rose toward its present unique importance in the world oil industry, British influence in the area underwent a step-by-step decline. Britain lost its primacy in Saudi Arabia to the United States after 1945, while continuing nevertheless to enjoy close relations with that kingdom. The nationalization of the Iranian oil industry in 1951 all but extinguished the traditional British influence in Iran. The overturn of the monarchy in Iraq seven years later brought to an end Britain's political and diplomatic paramountcy in that country. After 1958, to all intents and purposes British primacy in the Gulf had been reduced to the string of ministates on and off the Arabian coast.

In January 1968 the British Labor government, anxious to disengage from what remained of the British Empire, announced its intention to withdraw from the Persian Gulf within four years. It had foreshadowed this move only a month before by pulling out of the city of Aden and the more than 20 tribalities that made up the Protectorate of Aden (see the PDRY on map, page 18), where its attempt to establish a Federation of South Arabia had ended in a political shambles. Under British rule the city of Aden had grown into the largest bunkering port in the world, and had also become the site of a major refinery as a side effect of the Iranian oil crisis in the early 1950s. The hinterland, by contrast, had remained largely

Crated for departure, the British Royal Navy took its leave of Bahrain and the Persian Gulf in 1971, ending nearly a century and a half of British dominance over the Gulf.

Wide World Photos

unaffected by the British presence, since the Aden tribalities, like their Trucial replicas, were preclusive protectorates. The city of Aden, on the other hand, had attracted immigrants, mostly from northern Yemen, now the Yemen Arab Republic (YAR). Many became carriers of Arab radicalism; and after the British retirement they speedily seized power in the city and in the tribal hinterland, renaming the abortive federation the People's Democratic Republic of Yemen.

Britain's similar efforts to consolidate the Gulf tribalities into a viable federation met a better fate, largely because of the presence of monumental supplies of oil and the predicted exponential growth in the demand for it by the industrial consumers. On December 2, 1971, when Britain transferred power to the UAE, notes were exchanged with each successor state abrogating the agreements which, taken together, had constituted the British veiled-protectorate system. These were replaced by treaties of friendship whose only clause on military cooperation merely provided that the contracting parties should "consult together on matters of mutual concern in time of need."

Manifestly, Britain was unwilling to repeat the formula used a decade earlier in the comparable instrument signed with Kuwait, which had stipulated that "nothing . . . shall affect the readiness of Her Majesty's government to assist the government of Kuwait if the latter request such assistance." In less than a week after the conclusion of that treaty, Iraq had laid claim to Kuwait, which it charged had been stolen from Iraq by British imperialists. To forestall Iraqi military action, Britain flew some 600 marines to

Kuwait directly from England. The crisis was resolved peacefully and British military units were pulled out as units arrived from Saudi Arabia, the then United Arab Republic (Egypt and Syria) and Jordan, under the auspices of the Arab League. The stipulation of the 1961 agreement that provided for British military support on Kuwaiti request was annulled by mutual consent in March 1968.

Low Profile Military Connection

In the British election campaign of 1970, the Conservative party had pledged that it would not be bound by Labor's policy on the Persian Gulf. In office, however, the Conservative government found that the implementation of that policy had gone too far for reversal. Britain, therefore, evacuated on schedule its fewer than 8,500 officers and men in the British Forces Gulf Command. Nevertheless, the British remained discreetly but influentially involved in the armed forces of all the ministates. Officers, loaned by the British army, commanded the defense forces of Bahrain, Qatar and the UAE and even of Abu Dhabi, Dubai and Ras al-Khaimah, while other British officers and NCO's served under local contract. A smaller number of Jordanian officers and NCO's were also employed under contract by these minuscule armies.

Though in close relations with the United Kingdom, Oman had never formed part of the veiled-protectorate system in the Gulf. The sultanate had already concluded treaties with the United States (1833), France (1844) and the Netherlands (1877) by the time that Britain had extracted (1891) a nonalienation bond from the ruler. The British-Omani treaty relationship was not modified in 1971. British officers, NCO's and pilots were still loaned or contracted to the Omani Field Force under an agreement of July 1958, which also assured the Royal Air Force access to staging posts at Salalah in Dhofar province and on the island of Masirah, off the Omani coast.

Balanced Instability

According to most advance expectations, the moment the primary British props were removed in 1971, the regional structure in the Gulf should have collapsed. Yet at least until the 1978 convulsion in Iran, the successor structure seemed to be functioning. To be sure, marginal British supports remained. Britain helped keep the UAE alive, contributed to the durability of the regime in Qatar, and stiffened Oman's effort to contain a rebellion in its western province of Dhofar. Still, what remained was a far cry from the original system that Britain had so carefully erected in the 19th and early 20th centuries. Potentially, a more significant stabilizer in the emerging regional structure was the Arab League, whose members cultivated the practice of assisting in the mediation of disputes between Arab states. All the Arab states in the Gulf, large and small, belong to the League and also to the UN, which serve as sources of built-in regional and international support. Nevertheless, a fear of radicalization pervades the monarchical and quasi monarchical Gulf states, particularly in view of the seemingly irrepressible territorial disputes.

Long before the revolution in Iran, some already believed that political radicalization would be the inescapable outcome of the influx of foreign workers and fortune-seekers flocking to the oil-rich ministates of Kuwait, Qatar and Abu Dhabi. That this did not happen seems largely due to two factors. First, many are non-Arabs with no interest in Arab politics, seeking only to make money and go home. Second, although others are Arabs and, in many cases, potential radicalizers supported by their home governments or political movements to which they adhere, the Gulf rulers follow a policy of denying citizenship even to long-term foreign residents. This practice seems to have succeeded in holding such aliens in check so as to prevent their overwhelming the indigenous population.

The Egyptians in the Gulf have been a breed apart. In the 1950s and 1960s, Egyptian teachers staffed the burgeoning educational systems of the emirates and tribalities and carried a message of Arab unity through social revolution behind the banner of Gamal Abdel Nasser. Egyptians are still there, teaching at all levels from the primary schools through the universities, but they no longer speak with one voice, and their overall effect is becoming more and more conservative.

The Palestine Arabs, yet another pervasive strain up and down the Arabian side of the Gulf, promoted their resistance movement starting immediately after the 1967 war with Israel. But their preoccupation is the struggle with Israel and the search for material assistance in its conduct. Because of the generosity of the Arab oil states in support of the Palestine Arab cause, they have on the whole escaped the wrath of the Palestine Liberation Organization (PLO), the umbrella agency of the guerrilla groups.

Indigenous Radical Movements

Potentially more serious have been radicalizing movements indigenous to the Gulf or in its close proximity: the Ba'athi regime in Iraq, the civil war in Oman, and the vocal workers in Bahrain. Iraq's radicalization springs from the unstable politics of an unstable society. The recurrent military coups d'état have not enhanced the prestige or authority of the leaders. Ba'athi socialism has provided the slogans, but has hardly commended Iraq as a model to the traditional Gulf states. Indeed, Iraq quarrelled with every one of its neighbors in the Gulf and beyond until 1975, when it reached a *rapprochement* with Iran.

In Oman, what started out in Dhofar province in 1965 as a tribal dispute with the government later acquired ideological overtones, as Marxists from the neighboring PDRY after 1967 joined returning Omani exiles to infiltrate the rebel ranks. The Dhofaris are mountain tribesmen, scratching their subsistence from an unyielding soil. Such tribesmen are not easily drawn to abstract appeals, and their leaders could probably be converted into loyal subjects by enlightened sultanic policies of subventions and services. Instead, Sultan Qabus decided to suppress the uprising with his British-piloted air force, and later with help from Iran, Saudi Arabia and Jordan. By 1977 these forcible methods appeared to have brought the situation under control, but for how long none could tell.

Least attention has been given by outside observers to Bahrain, which in the early 1970s looked to some like the Gulf's front-running candidate for radicalization. It is the most literate mini-state, with the longest experience of development, and already had, by local standards, an articulate labor movement. These conditions combined with low oil income and limited opportunities for future growth suggest the desirability of close watching.

Territorial Disputes

More stubborn, in the short run, are the widespread territorial disputes, many arising from the absence of fixed frontiers. The European imperial powers imposed most present boundaries on the

Islamic world. Within the Arabian peninsula, firm and agreed frontiers have been defined only slowly, and the process is far from complete. The first peninsular boundaries were drawn in the north in the mid-1920s to fix the limits of Britain's mandates with the newly established Saudi kingdom, including the Iraqi-Saudi Neutral Zone. A second Neutral Zone between Saudi Arabia and Kuwait, a legacy of the same period, was divided between the two countries in 1969. In 1974 Saudi Arabia abandoned its claim to the Buraimi Oasis; in return, Oman agreed to the Saudi acquisition of an oil field and a corridor for a pipeline connecting that field to the Gulf. Elsewhere in the Arabian peninsular boundary, demarcation remains future business. Even Iraq and Iran, which concluded their major boundary agreement in 1937, did not fully settle their basic differences along the "agreed" dividing line until 1975.

The paucity of ironclad boundaries in an area flooded with such a highly prized liquid resource has created a lawyer's paradise among contentious neighbors. Deep-water oil drilling has extended territorial disputes into the waters of the Gulf. The riparian states have agreed to consider the Gulf their continental shelf, and have parceled out most of it by agreement. But where the claims of sovereignty crowd together, as at the head of the Gulf and among the islands in the south, the disputes are yet to be resolved.

Some territorial problems are aggravated not only by the cultural divide between the Arabs and the Iranians, but also by ideological tensions within the Arab fold. The radical Arab regimes have been plagued by violent disunity ever since the death in September 1970 of Nasser, who was able from time to time to unite them. Arab disunity would vanish quickly, however, if any non-Arab state—whether Iran or an interested extraregional power—should attempt to take vigorous action against an Arab state. This is the underlying meaning, for instance, of the Arab response to Iran's seizure in November 1971 of the Tunb Islands from Ras al-Khaimah and Abu Musa from Sharjah. Even those Arab governments in the Gulf friendly to Iran and the West were momentarily immobilized, as the Arab radicals traded on the crisis. Libya, one radical at some remove, promptly nationalized British Petroleum properties and concessions and severed relations with Britain, accusing it of complicity with Iran. Iraq, for its part, tried to build a reputation for selfless devotion to the Arab cause in the Gulf.

In fact, however, Iraq has been the regional maverick, antagonizing at one time or another all its neighbors in the Gulf. An example was its attempt in 1961, already described, to seize Kuwait. By this move it probably hoped to double its oil revenue and to acquire a good port directly on the Gulf. A second attempt to seize Kuwaiti territory occurred in 1973, when Iraqi troops crossed into the emirate to occupy the border police post of al-Samitah. The action was widely interpreted as a diplomatic tactic in "negotiating" the transfer to Iraq of the two Kuwaiti islands of Bubiyan and al-Warbah. Iraqi troops, deployed on Bubiyan for more than a year, had actually raised the Iraqi flag in December 1972. Possession of the islands would make access to the naval base at Umm Qasr less vulnerable and would substantially enlarge the Iraqi claim to a portion of the continental shelf. In 1973, as in 1961, the Arab League and individual Arab governments intervened to defuse the crisis before it became serious.

In July 1973 the foreign minister of Iraq publicly confessed that Iraq's security forces had erred in forcibly crossing the Kuwaiti border in March and disclosed that his government would seek a lease to the two islands, so as to assure secure transit to the naval base at Umm Qasr. In 1974–75, in a step of more lasting value—promising possible permanent relief from Iraqi adventurism in the future—an American company built for the Iraq National Oil Company the offshore deepwater terminal opposite the mud flats that make up the 35-mile Iraqi coast along the Gulf.

Iraq's later relations with Syria and Iran, following the downfall of the shah, will be examined below.

5

The Soviet Presence

In an earlier chapter, I noted that the U.S. interest in the Persian Gulf, aside from the critical importance of the region's oil resources, includes the responsibility for containing Soviet influence there. This responsibility was inherited from Britain at a moment when the United States, deeply embroiled in Vietnam, was ill-disposed to accept it. Yet the responsibility will not go away. In the present chapter I examine the Soviet Union's evolving position in the Gulf and nearby areas, and what it seems to imply for American interests.

To a Western eye viewing the affairs of the Persian Gulf, the Soviet Union is likely to be seen as an intruder. But intrusion is a matter of perspective. In the regional context, all outside powers seeking to take part in Gulf affairs might be viewed as intruders, unless they are Arab states. Even actions by outside Arab states appear intrusive to the government of Iran and at times, also, to one or more of its Arab neighbors in the Gulf.

In the international context of the mid-20th century, Britain had long since been installed in the Gulf. So, too, on a much more modest military scale, was the United States, after 1949, when it stationed the Middle East (Naval) Force at Bahrain. In the Anglo-American presence the world community acquiesced. By

1970, oil companies of U.S. nationality accumulated concessions or an interest in concessions for the development of close to 70 percent of the proved resources in the Gulf zone; companies of British nationality (in the case of Shell, with Dutch partners) fell well behind, with access to 20 percent. Companies of other extraregional nationality—principally French, Italian and Japanese—picked up much of the rest. Since 1970, however, all the states of the Gulf have shared in these operations through slow-motion nationalization of foreign concessions—a process euphemistically called participation.

The Soviet Union became an active participant in the Gulf zone's oil industry in 1969, when it sent technicians to Iraq to develop the North Rumailah oil field, then newly seized from the Western-owned Iraq Petroleum Company. In a three-year project, Soviet technicians sank the wells and built an 86-mile pipeline to the Gulf port of Fao, as well as storage tanks and docks for tankers.

Significantly, for this and other development assistance the Soviet Union did not seek, and was not given, a concession to the oil complex. Moscow advertised the activity, instead, as one of Iraqi national endeavor, unlike all the others in the Gulf zone, designed to enable local nationals to procure all the benefits of a nationalized segment of the domestic industry. Indeed, the Iraq National Oil Company, little more than a nominal company at the time that the Soviet aid program started, was brought to life as the owner, manager and operator of the North Rumailah-Fao complex by the deliberate Soviet policy of training Iraqis for the job. The Soviet Union did not buy all the crude pumped to Fao, nor did it act as the exclusive agent for its sale, as Western observers had widely expected. On the contrary, Moscow encouraged others to join it in buying the crude, and among the customers in the first year were French, Italian, Japanese and Kuwaiti oil companies, as well as those of Eastern Europe, India, Ceylon, Spain and Brazil.

The North Rumailah-Fao complex was opened with great flourish in April 1972. The high point of the ceremonies was the signing of a 15-year treaty of friendship and cooperation by Soviet Premier Alexei N. Kosygin and Iraqi President Ahmad Hassan al-Bakr. The treaty assures respect for the sovereignty of each party over its natural resources, condemns "imperialism in all its forms and manifestations," and pledges contact and coordination between

THE PERSIAN GULF

Major Oilfields 〰️〰️ Pipelines 〜

Airports ✈ Oil Terminals Ⓐ Ports <u>underlined</u>

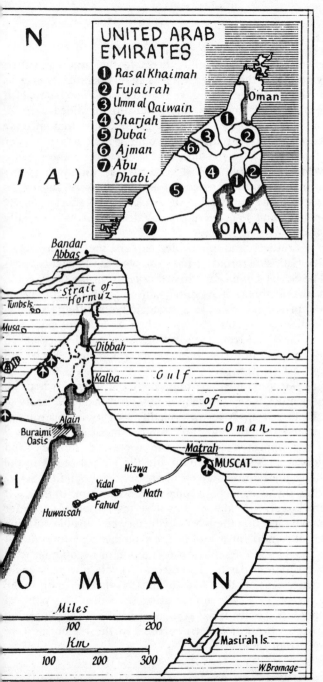

N

UNITED ARAB
EMIRATES

1 Ras al Khaimah
2 Fujairah
3 Umm al Qaiwain
4 Sharjah
5 Dubai
6 Ajman
7 Abu Dhabi

Oman

OMAN

I A)

Bandar Abbas

Strait of Hormuz

Tunbs Is.

Musa

Dibbah

Kalba

Gulf

of

Oman

Alain

Buraimi Oasis

Matrah

MUSCAT

Nizwa

Yidal
Nath
Fahud
Huwaisah

I

OMAN

Miles

100   200

Km

100   200   300

Masirah Is.

W. Bromage

From World Survey (London), January 1972

the two powers in the event of a threat to the peace of either.

The very novelty of the Soviet Union as an oil operator, or even as a technical adviser, in the Gulf gave rise to speculation, some of it wild, concerning Soviet motives. Some said this heralded a Soviet master plan for the seizure of all the oil in the Gulf—that once the tap was securely in its grasp, Moscow would be able to turn it on or off at will, forcing the Western industrial states to their knees. Since such a development would almost certainly precipitate war, any such Soviet intention may be ruled out as most unlikely. Indeed, its unreality is attested by the fact that the two great "oil shocks" felt by the West in 1973 and 1978 were precipitated by forces essentially independent of Soviet influence.

A more restrained, and plausible, explanation of the Soviet interest in the Gulf's oil resources has to do with Soviet energy needs at home. The Soviet Union, by importing oil from the Gulf, could accomplish several things: slow down consumption of its domestic oil resources, preserving them as a strategic reserve; bypass transportation bottlenecks within the sprawling Soviet landmass (for example, by moving oil from the Gulf through the Mediterranean to the Volga-Don industrial basin); or supplement Soviet oil deliveries to Eastern Europe.

A political purpose, however, may also be discerned when the Soviet-Iraqi venture is seen in conjunction with the 1972 treaty of friendship. By these steps Moscow evidently sought to win a voice in Gulf affairs and thereby end the "Anglo-American monopoly." Indeed, it has appeared to view the continued military and oil-concessionary presence of Britain and the United States in the Gulf as wholly undesirable. Given the secrecy surrounding Soviet policy-making, the assessment of long-term Soviet aims in the Gulf must remain largely speculative; but it seems reasonable to infer from the known facts that the most satisfactory conceivable outcome from the Soviet standpoint would be the same basic position that it has always sought elsewhere as a precondition of negotiation with the West: a position of parity. To reach that goal, however, would require a greater capacity than Moscow has yet shown—even in the Iranian events of 1978–79—for creating or controlling political events in the Gulf. Hence it has contented itself with encouraging and exploiting such anti-Western currents in the region as were available to it from time to time.

Prominent among Moscow's friends in the Arabian peninsula is 'Abdul Fattah Isma'il, a top leader in the People's Democratic Republic of Yemen whose strategically situated capital, Aden, was once a major British base.

Wide World Photos

One means to this end, of doubtful effectiveness, is an incessant stream of anti-Western radio propaganda beamed at the Gulf from the Soviet Union in local languages, even during periods of maximum détente with Washington, urging local governments to shake off their remaining connections with Britain, the United States and the Western oil companies. Another means is aid to subversive or dissident groups opposed to pro-Western governments. The main theater of this kind of operation has been the PDRY, whose Marxist leaders in Aden have had Soviet support in their sporadic wars against two neighbors—Oman's Dhofar province on the east and the conservative Yemen Arab Republic on the north. Neither enterprise has prospered. In Dhofar, the PDRY-inspired "insurrection" beginning in the 1960s drew British and Jordanian technicians and Iranian troops into the fighting, and pushed the Sultan of Oman into devoting nearly half of the sudden growth in his oil income—some $1.6 billion in 1977—to modernizing Oman's armed forces and paying for the war, which on the whole was going his way. This was hardly the result desired by Moscow. In February 1979 the new PDRY government, a faction loyal to Moscow rather than to China, opened a second front by invading the YAR—a move which caused alarm bells to ring in Washington and became the occasion for a new American show of firmness in the region.

The Soviet Union has also used more conventional diplomatic and economic means to project its influence among those governments of the region willing to deal with it. Its most intimate, though far from untroubled, relations have thus far been with Iraq. It also maintained correct diplomatic and close economic relations with Iran under the shah. Among the Arab states of the Arabian coast of the Gulf, the only state thus far to maintain formal diplomatic relations—along with minor trade relations—with the Soviet Union has been Kuwait.

Soviet Balancing Act

The Soviet Union's cultivation of relations with Iraq's often hostile neighbors, Iran and Kuwait, has led to unavoidable contradictions in Soviet diplomacy in the Gulf. As early as the mid-1960s, Moscow was issuing credits to Iran for economic projects which soon exceeded those given to Iraq. The most ambitious projects in Iran were a pipeline to bring natural gas to the Soviet Union from the southwestern oil fields, opened in 1970, and a steel mill in Isfahan, opened in 1973. For the Soviet Union, the investment brought a new source of fuel and a chance to loosen the dependence of imperial Iran on the United States—something the shah himself no doubt welcomed as a way to widen his diplomatic and economic options at minimum political risk. But the price Moscow paid was to become entangled on both sides of the Iraqi-Iranian controversy. On a smaller scale, Soviet relations with Kuwait caused a similar entanglement with that country and its hostile Iraqi neighbor.

Moscow's solution was to try in its own way to be evenhanded on all issues dividing the contestants. For example, starting in 1971, an Iraqi mission to the U.S.S.R. was often preceded or followed by an Iranian mission. Soviet Arabic-language broadcasts speak only of "the Arab Gulf" or "the Arabian Gulf," while Persian- and English-language programs refer to "the Persian Gulf." In 1971, Radio Moscow made no comments of its own either on Iran's seizure of the Arab islands of Abu Musa and the Tunbs or on Iraq's retaliatory severance of diplomatic relations with Britain and Iran.

It showed the same reticence when Iraq seized the Kuwaiti police post in 1973. In general, Iraq's abrasive relations with its neighbors, especially before 1975, made it a poor choice for the role of chief Soviet influence-projector in the region.

Related Areas: Israel and the Indian Ocean

In assessing the Soviet presence in the Gulf, and the ways in which it may bear upon U.S. interests, it is well to keep in mind that the Gulf cannot be isolated from related areas in the policy of either superpower. Soviet actions, actual or potential, concerning the Gulf are especially affected by the situation in two nearby areas of contention: the Arab-Israeli conflict and the nearer reaches of the Indian Ocean, especially the Arabian Sea and its littoral states in the Middle East and Africa. Although both these subjects lie outside the scope of the present study, it is useful to take note of the connection of each with Gulf affairs.

As to the Arab-Israeli dispute, for the purposes of this discussion, it may suffice to recall that all the oil states of the Gulf, except Iran, are members of the Arab League, and two of them, Saudi Arabia and Iraq, play leading roles in that organization. Although the two have commonly been on opposite sides in the League's tactical arguments over the Israel question—for example, Iraq has led the irreconcilable faction against Egypt's peace treaty with Israel, while Saudi Arabia has taken a middle position—both have a historically anti-Zionist posture, most recently shown in their endorsement of the March 1979 Baghdad resolutions imposing sanctions on Egypt. In addition, Iran as a newborn Islamic republic has strongly associated itself with the Arab position.

The significance of these facts for the position of the Soviet Union in the Gulf is tactical, not strategic, but it can be important. Soviet relations with, and opportunities for pressure on, the governments of the Gulf are likely to benefit, at least marginally, from any heightening of Arab hostility toward Israel and its chief protector, the United States. However, the Soviet Union's historic position of recognizing Israel, as well as its extreme wariness of any military confrontation with the United States, places clear limits on its opportunities to exploit the Israeli issue anywhere in the Arab world.

The link between the Gulf and the Indian Ocean is of a different kind. Here, a fact of direct significance in the strategic balance between the superpowers enters in. Soviet leaders must assume—Washington having always remained officially silent on the matter—that U.S. strategic missile submarines are on patrol beneath the waters of the Arabian Sea, which is the northwest corner of the vast Indian Ocean. From these waters, most of the Soviet industrial heartland, as well as Moscow, has fallen within the missile range of U.S. Polaris and Poseidon submarines. (The next-generation Trident submarine, with its longer-range missiles, will not need to go that close.)

Presumably it was this fact that accounted for the accumulation of Soviet political and military interests along the coastland from Aden to the Horn of Africa, in association with a considerable Soviet naval buildup in the Indian Ocean starting in 1968. The buildup proceeded despite the call of third world countries of the region, as early as 1970, to declare the entire area a "zone of peace" free of nuclear weapons. Since the reopening of the Suez Canal in 1976, Soviet naval access to the area has become much easier. The U.S. naval effort in the Indian Ocean, based mainly on the British atoll of Diego Garcia, was comparatively cautious until—as we shall see in the concluding chapter—the United States in 1979 began to respond with a show of naval strength designed primarily to reassure Saudi Arabia that an evident Soviet bid for increased influence in the region would not go by default.

As noted above, a Soviet attempt to interrupt the seaborne traffic in oil from the Gulf would be an act of war, and is thus highly improbable. Yet even an appearance of growth in the Soviet navy's capability to take such a drastic action—and, short of that, to project Soviet political influence in nearby East Africa—has had a further unsettling effect on the politics of the Gulf itself. In this sense, uneasiness over Soviet intentions and capabilities in the Indian Ocean cannot fail to interact with, and intensify, U.S. concern over political trends in the Gulf.

6

The Collapse of the Shah

As these words were written it was still far too early to gauge the ultimate direction of the Iranian revolution—or to seek to assess its impact on, or implications for, the remaining states washed by the Persian Gulf, their regional system, and the region's interplay with the world system. Yet it was already clear that the downfall of the pro-Western shah after a quarter of a century of undisputed power was a watershed in Iranian history, and an event whose repercussions, referred to in the opening chapter, were felt not in the Gulf alone but across the world.

Within Iran itself, in the early spring of 1979, the outcome of the revolution remained unclear. The Ayatallah Ruhallah Khomeini, who had come to symbolize the revolution while still in exile, retained the top leadership after his return to Iran in February. Khomeini set up a Council of the Islamic Revolution—widely known as the Komiteh—whose size and membership he did not disclose, to serve as the guardian of the religious interest in the transition to the projected Islamic republic. He then appointed Mehdi Bazargan, an engineer, former professor, and respected civil libertarian, as prime minister of a provisional government to oversee the affairs of state.

But no mutually accepted line of division was drawn between the religious and the secular. The ambiguity generated misunderstanding, tension and potential conflict between the Komiteh and the provisional government of Bazargan, who had been instructed to restore the country to normality. No one knew who held the power to deal with such urgent matters as the restoration of law and order; the reactivation of a paralyzed economy, particularly the oil industry; the conduct of external relations; the resuscitation of the armed forces and the redirection of their loyalty to the emerging regime; the oversight of the mass media; and the issuance of provisional legislation and the conduct of the courts.

At the end of March a national plebiscite brought a predetermined overwhelming majority vote for an Islamic republic. But on what lines the republic would be set up remained unclear. One of the many unanswered questions was how the provinces of the multi-ethnic state would be administered. For the Kurds, Baluchis, Turkmans and other tribal groups, the hope of the revolution had

Wide World Photos (pp. 40 & 41)

January 16, 1979: a somber-faced Mohammad Reza Shah Pahlavi walks to his airplane and into exile from the Iran he ruled for 25 years . . .

been to return not to Islam but to autonomy. Already the Iranian armed forces, much disorganized in the wake of the uprising, were challenged by tribal rebellion and claims to tribal self-government. If the Komiteh opted for centralism, might that not convert the tribal groups into rebels against the revolution? The longer the confusion lasted, the more troublesome would be the problems of reorienting the revolution to deal with the real problems of a society in ferment.

In the early months after the shah's departure these problems were aggravated by the erratic conduct of Ayatallah Khomeini, the symbol and hero of the revolution. Soon after his return to Iran, his irresolute and unsteady behavior underlined the familiar fact that leading a revolution and leading a government call upon different skills. Khomeini's lack of political experience—his naïveté, as some political observers called it—seemed to leave him, the Komiteh, the provisional government and the country itself bewildered about the new national goals and how to reach them.

...February 6, 1979: Ayatallah Ruhallah Khomeini, leader of the Islamic revolution that toppled the monarchy, holds audience with his newly appointed prime minister, Mehdi Bazargan.

41

Khomeini's problem was not simply personal. Underlying it was the fact that the Islamic role in Iran's revolution, while predominant, was not exclusive. Many other groups—the secular politicians of the National Front; Communists among the urban guerrillas of Tehran and among the strike organizers in the oil industry; intellectuals, students and women touched by the libertarian principles of the West; autonomy-seeking ethnic tribesmen—all these groups, each for its own reasons, joined in bitter opposition to the shah's police state. To bring it down, they accepted the lead of the *'ulama* (the professional men of religion), whose dominant voice was Khomeini. But once the shah went into exile and the remnants of his regime were swept away, the divergent purposes of the groups composing the revolution became manifest—and it was transformed overnight into a struggle for the succession to the monarchy, in which many groups progressively challenged the leadership of Khomeini and the 'ulama.

Iran's Revolution: How It Developed

The fear is widespread in the United States and Western Europe that the Islamic revolution in Iran is contagious and will speed across the Persian Gulf and perhaps even encompass the Muslim world. Such an outcome is possible but hardly probable. To understand the uniqueness of what has happened in Iran, let us probe a little further into the underlying causes and events of the revolution.

At the time of OPEC's doubling and redoubling of the price of crude oil in the last quarter of 1973, many experts believed that Iran stood the best chance among its oil-producing neighbors of using the huge revenues for the comprehensive modernization of its economy. With a population of more than 30 million, three times that of Iraq and twice that of all the Arab oil states of the Gulf combined, Iran was incontestably the region's superstate. Its technical and economic infrastructure, though still modest and uneven, was nevertheless more elaborate than that of any neighbor; for as early as 1963 the shah, with far smaller resources than those he would command a decade later, had launched a long-term "white revolution" to modernize his still nonindustrial kingdom and educate its largely illiterate people. The prospects that Iranians might fill most of the multiplying semiskilled and unskilled jobs in a rapidly diversifying economy seemed bright if the pace of economic expansion could be measured, not forced.

An impatient shah, however, tossed caution to the winds. With funds no longer wanting, he adapted his fifth development plan (ending in March 1978) to a strategy of instant modernization. He cultivated visions of transforming Iran into the world's fifth industrial power before the end of the century through a program of high-technology (capital-intensive not labor-intensive) development. This was, of course, sheer fantasy. Instant modernization yielded instant confusion. The sudden massive commodity and capital imports clogged the few harbors and the internal transportation system, which could not handle such a load. The strained distributive system, however, was the least socially disruptive and most easily correctable problem. To overcome local manpower shortages, workers were recruited from as far away as the Philippines and South Korea, as well as Afghanistan, Pakistan and India. The presence of thousands of foreigners added to social tensions. Yet even they were nowhere near as unsettling as the accelerated movement of Iran's own population from the villages to the towns, which churned up the society.

As in the other countries of the Middle East, the capital city lured more new settlers than any other cities, for that is where the action is in industry, commerce and finance and, for their children, in

Growth of the Six Major Cities in Iran as Shown in the Censuses of 1956, 1966 and 1976
(in thousands)

	1956	1966	Percentage of Growth	1976	Percentage of Growth	Percentage Growth 1956–76
Ahwaz	120	206	71	329	60	174
Isfahan	255	424	66	672	58	164
Mashhad	242	410	69	670	63	177
Shiraz	171	270	58	416	54	143
Tabriz	290	403	39	599	49	106
Tehran	1,512	2,720	80	4,498	65	197

Sources: United Nations, *Demographic Yearbooks* (1963, 1968 and 1977).

education at all levels. Tehran's population, estimated at about 500,000 in 1939, trebled by 1956, the date of the first census, and retrebled within 20 years, swelling to an estimated 5 million by 1978. By then, at least 75 percent of the Tehranis were peasants or children of peasants. The provincial towns replicated on a relative scale Tehran's experience. According to the 1976 census, Mashhad and Isfahan, with 670,000 each, shared second place. The population of both nearly trebled in 20 years as had also that of Ahwaz, the capital of Iran's principal oil-producing province, while the population of Shiraz and Tabriz more than doubled. (See table p.43.)

The new townsmen found employment but no proper housing. The government could neither build the new houses that were needed nor immediately furnish community services such as water, electricity, paved streets and schools. As the slums spread out and the conditions of crowding worsened, the internal immigrants progressively lost their rural cohesion without, as a rule, satisfying their exaggerated expectations.

Everywhere, in the capital and the provinces, most of the semiurbanized townsmen remained practicing Muslims. They responded warmly to the appeals of the 'ulama, who paid greater attention than the government to the urgent needs of the erstwhile villagers.

Meanwhile, after 1972, the shah adopted a strategy of instant military modernization, parallel to his economic program with the same emphasis on high technology. When the shah had been reinstated in August 1953, the armed forces consisted of 126,000 officers and men. By 1960 the size of the total establishment had enlarged to 202,000. In the next dozen years, chiefly on American insistence, the armed forces were reduced to 191,000; only the air force gradually expanded to 22,000.

After 1972 the military establishment underwent unprecedented growth. The ranks of the army rose to 285,000 in 1978; the navy more than trebled to 28,000, while the air force zoomed to 100,000 by 1977. The shah in his haste had apparently abandoned his earlier practice of slow officer promotion, based as much on political loyalty as on merit. This lapse in caution went a long way toward explaining, in the 1978 crisis that deposed the shah, the early defection of the air force to the revolutionaries, and the later disintegration of the ground forces.

The investment in military hardware outpaced by far the growth in military manpower. Between 1945 and 1972, Iran had spent a total of $1.2 billion on arms imports. Over the next half-dozen years, the shah entered into commitments for the purchase of more than $18 billion worth of weapons, among them some of the most sophisticated systems in the inventories of the United States and its Western European allies—including F-14 Tomcat fighters with Phoenix air-to-air missiles that give the fighter its 100-mile reach, P-3F Orion antisubmarine patrol planes, Chieftain tanks, Spruance-class destroyers, and the AWACS (airborne warning and control system), a plane which even major allies of the United States found too expensive.

The shah was able to do this because the United States in May 1972 had agreed to sell him virtually any conventional military hardware he wanted. That decision was taken by President Richard M. Nixon and his national security adviser, Henry A. Kissinger—at a time, it should be noted, before anyone foresaw the monumental rise in the price of crude oil that was about to take place in less than 20 months, placing in the shah's hands more money than he could have anticipated in his wildest dreams. It proved a rash decision which lifted all normal U.S. restraints on the transfer of the most advanced conventional weapons to third world countries.

These developments by no means exhaust the list of the politically explosive materials that were accumulating in the shahdom in the years of forced development. In a rapidly expanding society, with a majority of the population 20 years old or younger, the universities grew into centers of activism, as they came to symbolize the hope of the future in overcoming the burdens of widespread illiteracy. The University of Tehran, in particular, developed into the headquarters for almost every movement of protest against the shah—religious and secular, Communist and free-enterprise, pro-Soviet and pro-Chinese, Trotskyite and Maoist, urban guerrilla and civil libertarian. Because of the outspoken condemnation of the police state by students and faculty, the government again and again shut the universities for varying periods, but the resistance instead of fading away grew ever more stubborn.

Moreover, in the decade and a half of the shah's "white revolution," a new class of professionals arose (including many of the technocrats employed in planning and managing the accelerated

Exodus: Scores of thousands of American and European executives, technicians, and their families, working in Iran on military and industrial projects financed by post-1973 oil riches, left the country in late 1978 when agitation against the monarchy took a sharply anti-Western turn.

economic plans), most of them trained abroad and exposed to Western ideas of political and civil liberties. An able and intelligent group, they were bound to resent the personal wealth that accumulated among the shah's favorites, in which few of them shared, and bound also to clash with the shah's political repression.

There were also in the urban areas the old-style merchants of the bazaars, who grew steadily richer as Iran prospered but who remained distrustful of the shah and his policies and faithful to the 'ulama. As the government took away from the 'ulama accustomed sources of revenue, such as many of the religious endowments and royal subsidies, the bazaaris made up the deficiencies with their new-found wealth.

Furthermore, the ethnic, linguistic and sectarian communities remained as a potential threat to Iran's cohesion. To be sure, there was no open evidence, even at the end of the shah's rule, of restiveness—to say nothing of a reawakened urge to separatism—among these communities; but the alacrity with which they began asserting their autonomy after the collapse of the monarchy left little doubt of their continuing resentment of centralized authority.

Above all, there were the 'ulama themselves, the religious

establishment of Shi'ah Islam, the dominant religion in Iran. Status in this establishment extends from the rank-and-file *mullas* (trustees of the faith), to the learned *mujtahids* (interpreters of the faith) at the centers of religious instruction and in positions of religious authority in the cities and towns, to the handful of mujtahids who styled themselves ayatallah (sign of Allah), a relatively recent honorific title (the equivalent of "excellency" in the religious establishment in a title-ridden country), to Khomeini himself, who after reaching France in October 1978 allowed himself to be called *imam* (supreme leader, a title which among the Shi'ites of Iran is commonly reserved for the messiah). At all ranks, the 'ulama were bound to see in the shah's imperial modernizing, with its secular focus, a direct challenge to their authority. Still revered by the practicing Shi'ites and increasingly a solace to the disoriented peasants in the towns and cities, the estimated 180,000 men of religion became the mobilizers of protest and, ultimately, of revolution.

To these gathering forces of resistance the shah's answer was threefold. He sought to outweigh them by the new military and economic classes which he rapidly created, and to whom he looked for loyalty. He sought to inspire and awe them with a cult of personality built around his imperial person and the ancient, pre-Islamic Persian heritage of kingly rule. Finally, what he could not outweigh or inspire he sought to repress through the all-too-familiar apparatus of the police state. His secret police, known as SAVAK, became for the opposition the most hated force in Iran. The list of political dissidents abroad lengthened. Among them was Ayatallah Khomeini, long an outspoken foe of the shah, who since 1964 had been living in Iraq as an exile in the Shi'ite shrine city of al-Najaf.

Until 1977 there were no untoward signs that the shah's system was in danger. The first symptom of possible internal disorder, visible in retrospect, was his sudden, unexplained dismissal in August 1977 of the government of Prime Minister Amir 'Abbas Hoveida after a dozen years in office. But that was, at the time, only a faint symptom, since replacement of governments had been common until the start of the shah's "white revolution" in 1963. Indeed, many wondered why the Hoveida cabinet had lasted as long as it had.

The first overt sign of serious opposition, and of its probable source, came in January 1978. Out of a blue sky the government had inspired the publication of a letter accusing Ayatallah Khomeini, then in his 14th year of exile, of collaborating with Communists in a conspiracy to overthrow the Iranian monarchy. On January 9, in reply to the letter, opponents of the shah staged a protest demonstration in the shrine city of Qum. Although the demonstrators were met with force, the opponents of the shah grew progressively bolder as 1978 wore on. In November the shah appointed the chief of staff, General Gholam Riza Azhari, prime minister of the third government of the year which composed six other military officers and four civilian technicians. Martial law, first imposed on the major cities on September 8, continued in effect until the end of the imperial regime. Meanwhile Khomeini, who had moved to France in October, assembled around him aides to coordinate the mass protests in Iran demanding that the monarchy give way to an Islamic republic. As the insurgents gathered strength in defiance of the heavily armed security forces, the shah's successive measures of compromise—including appointment of a respected opponent, Shahpur Bakhtiar, as prime minister, and the arrest of persons accused of profiteering—came too late to do more than sap the credibility of the monarchy and whet the appetites of his foes for complete victory. On January 16, 1979 the royal family fled from Iran; on February 1, Khomeini returned in triumph to Tehran; and on February 11, the Bakhtiar interregnum collapsed.

Is 'Khomeini Fever' Catching?

Against this background, let us return to the question whether what has been called Khomeini fever might, as many fear, infect other states in the region of the Gulf.

In this writer's opinion, such a development is unlikely. Apprehension over it stems largely from a supposition that, since all rich oil states have sought instant modernization, the consequences will be uniform. But in important respects the conditions that produced revolution in Iran are not present, or are much less prominent, in the conservative Arab monarchies and sheikhdoms of the Arabian peninsula.

To begin with, among the Arab states of the Gulf there has been no parallel to the massive movement of Iran's population from countryside to city. The oil-producing ministates, in fact, simply do not have the people to redistribute. The reshuffling of their sparse populations from village or desert to town does indeed alter the migrants' way of life, but without necessarily producing social catastrophe, since the governments—unlike that of Iran under the shah—take care to distribute patronage and favors among all the citizens.

More unsettling has been the presence of steadily swelling foreign communities, of mixed ethnic and linguistic origins, which in some of the ministates have come to outnumber the original population. However, all these groups are denied citizenship—even those who have immigrated from the oil-dry Arab states such as North Yemen. They hardly constitute a political challenge to the regimes and are seldom, if ever, advocates of social or religious radicalism.

Much anxiety centers on Saudi Arabia, the chief power of the region next to Iran and the first among the oil earners of the Gulf. It shows symptoms of forced-pace social change midway between those of Iran and those of the peninsular ministates. However, Saudi demographic problems are less severe than those of Iran. Its urban centers may also be swollen with uprooted peasant and bedouin; but in many towns the influx consists of at least as many foreign workers, who, though numerous, pose little political threat. The largest foreign resident community, an estimated 1 million Yemenis—nearly 20 percent of the population of Saudi Arabia—creates more problems for the YAR than for the host country. The Yemenis would rather earn good wages as unskilled workers in Saudi Arabia than be drafted into the armed forces of their embattled country.

Nor is the Saudi system of government as inherently vulnerable as that created by the shah. The absolutism of the shah rested on repression and a cult of personality. In Saudi Arabia, what counts is less the incumbent on the throne than the rulership of the extended royal family and their ability to work as a cohesive group. This collegial system survived the shock of the assassination of King Faisal in 1975, and has encouraged the rise of its most talented members to the positions of leadership. The tension in the system is mounting, however, among the politically active princes—particularly between the founder's sons, who had at best only a traditional education, and his grandsons who were educated in the West, mostly in the United States.

A further potential political weak spot is the Saudi army. The shift now under way from the old tribal force or White Army, which until the early 1970s had served as the primary instrument of domestic security, to a modernized army whose loyalty has yet to be tested, does raise questions about the future. It is also doubtful that the sophisticated weapons systems the Saudi military have acquired can be assimilated effectively by such a small military establishment. Even if they can, it is more doubtful still that such a modern army would provide the regime greater security—whether against foreign or domestic foes—than it has enjoyed in the past. Still, a reversal of the arms-transfer policies would have to be negotiated with supreme tact and with no certitude of success.

In sum, Saudi Arabia's political system appears far less fragile than was the autocracy of the Pahlavi dynasty in Iran, but it is by no means invulnerable to the shocks of modernization or to the fears and dangers arising from shifting power alignments in and around the Gulf. Its future may thus depend as much on external as on internal factors.

The Arab-Israeli Factor

Of all external political factors, none has been more troublesome to relations between the United States and the Arab states of the Gulf than the Arab-Israeli conflict. Historically, the division among the members of the Arab League between radicals and moderates on the Israel question has also manifested itself in the Gulf, with Iraq generally among the irreconcilables and Saudi Arabia—despite its strong religious attitude on the issue of Muslim rights in Jerusalem—taking a generally moderate stand in deference to its established American connection. So long as the conflict persists, it will continue to disturb the politics of the entire Arab world, including those of the Gulf. The oil sanctions imposed by the Organization of Arab Petroleum Exporting Countries (OAPEC) in 1973 gave dramatic proof of this.

Arab solidarity against Israel's position in the West Bank and the Gaza Strip was demonstrated anew after Egyptian President Anwar el-Sadat made his dramatic visit to Jerusalem in November 1977, and once again in the wake of the Camp David accords of

September 1978, when it became evident that bilateral peace between Israel and Egypt might be imminent. A conference in Baghdad in November 1978, attended by all members of the Arab League except Egypt, with many represented by their heads of state, adopted a resolution branding as a breach of Arab solidarity President Sadat's endorsement of the Camp David framework for agreement. This and other resolutions were clearly framed to discourage Sadat from concluding a separate peace treaty with Israel and to reaffirm that the Arab interest could be safeguarded only in a comprehensive settlement.

While all the Arab oil states of the Gulf opposed Sadat's diplomacy, the bases of their opposition were hardly uniform. On the quarrel with Israel, Iraq has remained an implacable hardliner, a position reinforced by the fact that its friend, the Soviet Union, had been bypassed in the 16 months of U.S. mediation of the Egyptian-Israeli negotiations. Moreover, Iraq—alone among the Gulf states—joined the Steadfastness and Confrontation Front established by Algeria, Libya, Syria, the PDRY and the Palestine Liberation Organization in December 1977. Iraq took this step on the eve of the Baghdad conference, after having at first rejected the front's program as much too lenient.

Saudi Arabia and the ministates, on the other hand, with Jordan in tow, had refused to associate themselves with the categorical dismissal of Sadat's diplomatic initiatives. They tended instead to take a middle position. The leading consensus-seeker in Arab regional politics, the Saudi Arab government, expressed unhappiness and even anger over Sadat's visit to Jerusalem and later diplomacy because of his failure to consult the other members of the Arab League in advance. Even more outspokenly critical of the Egyptian president was the government of Kuwait, a sensitivity explained by the high proportion—at least 20 percent and perhaps more—of Palestinians in its population. Yet neither Saudi Arabia nor Kuwait withheld or reduced its subsidies to Egypt. Nor did the two governments interrupt their contributions to the Gulf Organization for the Development of Egypt, which they established along with the United Arab Emirates and Qatar in 1977 to funnel large-scale grant aid to Egypt.

Immediately following the ceremony in Washington, at which Israeli President Menahem Begin, President Jimmy Carter and

Sadat signed the instruments of an Egyptian-Israeli peace, the Arab League Council at the level of foreign, economic and finance ministers reconvened in Baghdad on March 27-31, 1979 to put into effect the punitive measures proposed by the Arab summit nearly five months earlier. These included the severance of political and diplomatic relations with Egypt; the suspension of its membership in the League; the temporary transfer of the League headquarters from Cairo to Tunis; the promotion of the suspension of Egypt's membership in the third-world Nonaligned Conference, the Islamic Conference Organization and the Organization of African Unity; the stoppage of economic aid and of the sale of oil to Egypt; and the application of an economic boycott against Egyptian firms, institutions, and individuals entering into dealings "directly or indirectly with the Zionist enemy." These resolutions, approved by all Arab states in the Gulf except Oman, were put into prompt effect. Still, the resolutions distinguish between punishing those Egyptians who cooperated with Sadat's peace policies and safeguarding the Arab interest in the welfare of the Egyptian people. Through this loophole, there continued to flow each month an estimated $150 million in private remittances from Egyptian workers in the Arab oil states.

The drama of these periodic Arab declarations and actions against Israel is above all the drama of Saudi Arab diplomacy. That country faces no more difficult a diplomatic task than that of maintaining a degree of Arab solidarity in times of crisis over Israel while still keeping in repair its vital connection with Israel's chief protector, the United States. In 1973, for a time, this proved impossible, but the interruption was brief. Will it be brief again in 1979?

Who Shall Lead in the Gulf?

The United States, after Britain's departure from the Gulf in 1971, deliberately chose not to succeed Britain as the paramount power in the Gulf. Instead, there emerged the policy of "twin pillars"—Iran and Saudi Arabia—as the leading regional powers, each backed by the United States and plentifully supplied with the weapons which both could later afford to buy in abundance. Of the twin pillars, the larger by far, and the bigger customer for military hardware, was Iran.

The downfall of the monarchy in Iran ended that system, plunged the chief power of the region into chaos, and thus created a power vacuum in the Gulf. There was still no generally accepted governmental authority in the country at the time of writing, and little prospect that one would take shape in the near future. Without it, the reconstitution of the military establishment as a credible force remained little more than a pious hope. In the interval no other neighboring state could replace Iran. The Saudi defense budget, admittedly, soared nearly as high as that of Iran, each ranging from $7.5–$8 billion in 1977, and from $9.5–$10 billion a year later. But with a population and a military establishment only one-seventh those of Iran, Saudi Arabia could hardly contemplate taking over Iran's regional security role. A comparison of the military expenditures of the two countries (see table p.13) underlines the differences. Iran invested most heavily in the latest sophisticated hardware and in military industry, in the obvious expectation of achieving military autarky at an early date. Saudi Arabia also bought the most modern conventional hardware; but its overall purchases were scaled to the size of a much smaller military establishment. Moreover, it set aside the largest sums for military infrastructure, such as camps, roads and telecommunications. Nor could Saudi Arabia envision the creation of a substantial military industry. Instead, in May 1975 it joined Qatar, the UAE and Egypt in creating the Arab Organization for Industrialization to make or assemble in Egypt a wide range of military hardware, from helmets to jeeps and missiles, partly under American, British and French contracts. The oil partners invested $1.4 billion in the consortium while Egypt provided the workers.

Still less can Iraq be looked to as the Gulf's future leader. With 12.5 million people, Iraq is the most populous Arab state on the Gulf. By 1978 its armed forces had doubled in five years to 212,000, and its military budget quintupled to nearly $1.7 billion. But in a region where all the other Arab governments are fundamentally frightened of radicalism, particularly of the Communist variety, Iraq as a close friend of the Soviet Union could not look ahead to winning the trust of its oil-producing Arab neighbors.

To sum up: In the afterlight of the Iranian conflagration, the Arab states of the Gulf—especially Saudi Arabia and the oil sheikhdoms—seem considerably less vulnerable to internal overthrow than was the imperial regime of the Iranian shah. External security, however, is another matter. The Gulf is connected to the world and its insecurities by certain enduring facts: its vast oil treasure, its proximity to the Soviet Union and the Indian Ocean, and its Arab involvement in the conflict with Israel. Such facts are of great concern to the United States and its allies. With the Gulf security system that Washington built so largely around the shah of Iran now in ruins, and no local successor to Iran in sight, the United States faces new questions about its policy toward the important region. To these questions I now turn.

7

The Search for New Policies

For all the public theorizing over U.S. foreign policy, the actual making of it often seems less a matter of systematic planning than of improvisation and drift. So it has been at times in policy on the Persian Gulf. After the British withdrawal, U.S. policy was keyed to the habit of British-American partnership, a relic of an earlier period when the special relationship between the two allies encircled the globe. The United States took no dramatic initiatives; it was reactive, not creative. Its most daring action—or inaction— was to keep, and modestly modernize, the small naval Middle East Force in Bahrain.

The overriding concern behind the British-American policy of those years was to keep the oil flowing—and, hence, to defend the Gulf against Soviet penetration. The concern was justified, but its focus was too narrow. As we learned in 1973, policy-makers interested in the assured flow of oil should have paid greater attention than they did, beginning in 1970, to the steady transfer of power from the multinational oil companies to the governments of the major oil-exporting states of the Gulf. Having failed to give this development due weight, no Western government was ready for the energy crisis when it broke—still less for its manifold conse-quences.

The Hidden Balancer

Among those consequences was the sudden enrichment of the oil exporters. Luckily for the United States and its allies, the greatest oil wealth flowed into conservative hands in Saudi Arabia and Iran. Both powers were as ready to convert this wealth into political and military power as Washington was to help them do so, thus recycling petrodollars back into the U.S. economy and also laying the foundations of a new security structure in the Gulf. From this set of facts unfolded the so-called twin pillars policy, in which the flow of modern military equipment and training in its use was combined with U.S. diplomatic support within the region and beyond. The two governments were assumed to be internally stable. With the quiet backing of the United States and its allies (most commonly Britain and Jordan), they were counted on to check the radical governments of Iraq and the PDRY, and to keep the ministates from falling prey to radicalism.

Drift or no drift, the policy worked for seven years, maintaining at least a surface stability in the Gulf that many in advance had thought impossible. The rewards were substantial. Saudi Arabia in March 1974 ended the Arab oil embargo, imposed in the Arab-Israel war five months earlier. All other Arab oil producers acquiesced in the Saudi initiative. For five years after December 1973 OPEC, despite the steady decline of the dollar for which oil is sold, raised the price of crude oil only once, in 1976. This was largely due to the cooperation of Saudi Arabia, which, with its excess capacity to take up any slack in production, stood firm against pressures, including those from Iran, to force the price up. Meanwhile Iran, although a "hawk" on the oil-price question, became America's chief arms customer and seemed in most ways to prosper under the shah's autocratic rule. And, with help from the twin pillars, minor outbreaks of radicalism, chiefly from the PDRY, were effectively contained.

In all this, the United States played the part of the hidden balancer. Because of the mood of Congress and the American public, this was perhaps the only policy available to Washington at the time: one of low visibility, low cost and low risk.

New Circumstances, Old Interests

Now one of the twin pillars is down, and the seven-year U.S.

U.S. Oil Imports from the Persian Gulf
(thousand barrels per day)

	1972		1977	
Iran	141.8		535.0	
Iraq	3.6		73.7	
Saudi Arabia	189.6		1,386.4	
Bahrain	14.8		9.5	
Kuwait	44.8		48.1	
Oman	0.068		82.2	
Qatar	3.5		66.5	
United Arab Emirates	73.4		335.3	
		Percentage of U.S. Daily Consumption:		Percentage of U.S. Daily Consumption:
Total Persian Gulf Imports	471.6	2.88	2,536.7	13.76
Total U.S. Imports	4,741.3	28.97	8,807.2	47.79
Daily Consumption	16,367.0		18,431.0	

Sources: U.S. Department of Interior, Bureau of Mines, *Mineral and Industry Surveys,* "Crude Petroleum, Petroleum Products and Natural-Gas-Liquids: 1972," prepared in the Division of Fossil Fuels, December 21, 1973; U.S. Department of Energy, Energy Information Administration, *Energy Data Reports,* "Supply, Demand and Stocks of All Oils by P.A.D. Districts and Imports into the United States by Country: Final 1977," prepared in the Office of Energy Data and Interpretation, February 8, 1979.

policy of the invisible balancer, working through compatible powers in the area, is called into question. But the interests the United States must protect in the Gulf are still the same: oil, Arab moderation toward Israel, and a balance to Soviet penetration and influence. Let us briefly examine each of these interests as matters stood in early 1979.

Oil. The uprising against the monarchy in Iran was accompanied by oil workers' strikes which halted exports altogether for more than two months. It was the second time in five years that the flow of Gulf oil had been interrupted for political reasons. In both instances, the shortfall enabled OPEC to raise its prices for crude oil.

The tragedy is that the United States, still without a realistic energy program, was as ill prepared for the second interruption as it had been for the first. In effect, this country wasted the five-year respite obtained by its twin-pillars diplomacy. Three successive American presidents did not go far enough to explain to the public the extreme vulnerability of American and allied essential supplies. The Congress responded, not to the future dangers of oil vulnerability, but to the present wishes of constituents. As far back as the start of the 1970s, some oil companies, but by no means all, began warning the public about the implications of the mounting reliance on a wasting resource. Other oil companies, however, lost none of their preoccupation with profits. Without clear and vigorous leadership, the public made little more than feeble efforts to reduce consumption. There were no realistic guidelines on conservation, exploration, pricing, or research and development for alternative forms of energy. Instead of operating to remove the causes of the infection, the United States was putting Band-Aids on the multiple

sores. Whether the Carter Administration's new oil policy of April 1979 heralded a more serious attack on the vital problems could not be foreseen at this writing.

The need for governmental leadership is clear. The major oil companies devote important efforts to improving methods for recovering more of the oil from reserves already discovered, and to exploration for new resources within the United States and its continental shelves. Individual companies also engage in research on alternative forms of energy, partly with support from the U.S. Department of Energy. But the separate research programs of individual companies lack overall coordination and thus do not fit into any comprehensive program with clear goals. Besides, in view of the antitrust constraints on the companies, only the Federal government can provide the necessary coordination and stimulus.

Israeli-Arab dispute. There is a direct interplay between the Egyptian-Israeli negotiations launched by President Sadat in November 1977 and the palliative politics of energy in the United States. It was continued U.S.—and European and Japanese—dependence on the Gulf's oil, more than the fundamental urgency of an Arab-Israeli settlement, that explained the concentration of a busy American president on the slow-motion Sadat-Begin bazaar bargaining, and the full American role in the instruments signed in March 1979. In the next phase of the peace-seeking process, the United States faced the need to convince the skeptical governments of the Gulf's oil states that the Egyptian-Israeli treaty was only the first major step toward a comprehensive settlement. Given the wide chasm separating the two sides on the Palestinians, Jerusalem and other issues, it seemed a near-impossible task. Yet it must be done without undermining Israel's security, if for no other reason than the undiminished U.S. dependence on the oil of the Gulf.

Balancing the Soviet Union. The Gulf's oil exporters (except Iraq) and the industrial importers have long shared a fear of the spread of radicalism in the Gulf. Although the source of radical movements may be as much Islamic (as in Iran) as Communist, it is the hand of the Soviet Union that is most feared, and not without reason.

The concern is much wider now than in 1971-72, when it was chiefly the newly independent ministates that were thought most vulnerable. By 1978-79, in the wake of the events in Iran, the anxiety is over the basic question of the reestablishment of a "stable" interstate system in the Gulf. Linked with this is the ominous question of Saudi Arab confidence in the United States.

Until the latest crisis, the United States still enjoyed the basic trust of the Saudi leaders. But the Saudi belief in America's will to use its power had already begun to waste away because of the passivity of the Carter Administration toward the renewed fighting in the Dhofar province of Oman in 1978 and the Soviet advances in the Horn of Africa. The culminating shock was the downfall of the shah. The succession of nonpolicies toward these challenges, as seen in Riyadh and the ministate capitals, undermined the credibility of the United States. The precipitous decline in American prestige created many problems for the United States and for the Arab oil rulers. How should the rulers plan their own future security if they could no longer lean on a friendly superpower? Should they proclaim, as the Islamic leadership of Iran was doing, that they would pursue an external policy of nonalignment?

Evidently receiving this signal of Saudi concern, the Carter Administration in March 1979 shifted abruptly from near total inaction to hyperaction toward the multiplying crises in and around the Gulf. Contrast the following:

In December 1978, a carrier task force was detached from the Seventh Fleet in the western Pacific for temporary duty in the Arabian Sea—only to have the order rescinded before its execution. In January 1979, there appeared in Saudi Arabia a squadron of 12 unarmed F-15s for five days of "maneuvers"—evoking more ridicule than respect.

But starting on March 6, the Department of Defense prominently advertised the sailing from Subic Bay in the Philippines for the Arabian Sea of a task force composing a battle-equipped aircraft carrier with a full complement of fighters, attack, antisubmarine and reconnaissance planes together with a cruiser and a destroyer. The force arrived at its destination ten days later for indefinite deployment, and by mid-April a second carrier task force entered Indian Ocean waters on parallel assignment. Meanwhile, two advanced American surveillance planes had reached Saudi Arabia on March 9 for special duty to observe air action over the battle zone in the YAR and to follow the movement of Soviet supply planes to the PDRY.

At the same time, the United States concluded an agreement with Saudi Arabia, at the latter's cost, to airlift to the YAR military aid valued at close to $400 million. Along with the hardware went "mobile training teams," which were expected to number some 230 men within a few weeks, eventually rising even higher. American technicians in Saudi Arabia, including maintenance crews for the fighter planes, supplemented the teams in the YAR. In taking this decision, President Carter invoked the waiver clause of the Arms Export Control Act to avoid congressional review—thus signaling "an emergency" affecting "the national security interests of the United States." By the time of arrival of the first equipment on March 17, the Arab League Council had already negotiated a ceasefire between the two Yemens. The aid program, however, remained unchanged. Clearly, the presidential decision, with all its implications for the possible future avoidance of congressional oversight, had to be weighed on the larger regional scales.

A Visible Balancer?

The simultaneous deployment of two carrier task forces established a precedent, although at intervals in recent years, a single such force had been sailing into the Indian Ocean and the Arabian Sea. Also new was the serious talk in the Pentagon of the creation of a Fifth Fleet for continuous service in the Indian Ocean. If such a decision were taken, the U.S. Navy might be expected to appeal to Congress for the construction of more ships and for the further enlargement of the support facilities in those waters—since the existing facility on Diego Garcia has no major repair yards, although it can accommodate land-based antisubmarine planes, fuel storage and spare parts.

The sudden sharp rise in the U.S military profile in and near the Gulf served to warn the Soviet Union and its allies against further probes so close to vital American and Western interests; to neutralize the criticism of U.S. passivity by Saudi Arabia and the ministates; and to salvage American influence in the Persian Gulf so as to enable the United States to resume a constructive stabilizing role.

In a word, the show of force was designed to demonstrate U.S. willingness to act as a visible, instead of merely an invisible, balancer in the interstate system of the Gulf. The visible balancer's lot, if Washington decides to accept it, will be a busy one. The balancer will have to do what it can to uphold, when challenged, the Saudi monarchy and the quasi monarchies of the ministates; to protect the struggle for the succession in Iran against external meddling; and to reassure the Arab oil states that the Arab interest in the negotiating process toward a comprehensive settlement of the conflict with Israel, and now also in the quarrel with Egypt, will be fairly accommodated.

Talking It Over

A Note for Students and Discussion Groups

This pamphlet, like its predecessors in the HEADLINE Series, is published for every serious reader, specialized or not, who takes an interest in the subject. Many of our readers will be in classrooms, seminars or community discussion groups. Particularly with them in mind, we present below some discussion questions—suggested as a starting point only—and references for further reading.

Discussion Questions

What lessons for U.S. foreign policy do you see in the overthrow of the royal government in Iran? Do you agree or disagree with the author's assessment that similar turbulence is unlikely in other countries of the Gulf? Explain your view.

What were the main lines of U.S. policy in the Gulf after Britain laid down its paramountcy and until the overthrow of the shah of Iran? What historical factors shaped this policy and inhibited Washington from playing a more direct role?

Why did the Soviet Union become interested in the Gulf? How would you describe major Soviet aims in the Gulf? Do you think that Soviet policy and behavior in the Gulf are compatible with its espousal of détente with the United States?

Do you think the United States should or should not establish a strong and recognized naval presence in the Indian Ocean? Why or why not?

The author discusses three distinct ways in which U.S. interests are involved in the affairs of the Gulf. How would you rank these interests in order of importance? Discuss.

Do you agree with the author's view that reducing U.S. dependence on Persian Gulf oil imports is important enough to justify the economic sacrifices required?

Do you believe the stakes in maintaining political stability in the Gulf justify whatever risks the United States may run in a new effort, following the fall of the shah, to serve as the "visible balancer" of power in the area?

READING REFERENCES

Amirie, Abbas, ed., *The Persian Gulf and Indian Ocean in International Politics.* Tehran, Institute for Political and Economic Studies, 1975.

Anthony, John Duke, *Arab States of the Lower Gulf: People, Politics, Petroleum.* Washington, The Middle East Institute, 1975.

Bill, James A., "Iran and the Crisis of '78." *Foreign Affairs,* Winter 1978/79.

Burrell, R. M., *The Persian Gulf.* The Washington Papers, No. 1. Washington, Center for Strategic and International Studies of Georgetown University, 1972.

Chubin, Shahram, and Zabih, Sepehr, *The Foreign Relations of Iran: A Small State in a Zone of Great-Power Conflict.* Berkeley, University of California Press, 1974.

Hurewitz, J. C., "The Persian Gulf: British Withdrawal and Western Security." *Annals of the American Academy of Political and Social Science,* May 1972.

Ivanov, K., "The U.S.S.R. and the Persian Gulf." *Mizan,* March-April 1968.

Khadduri, Majid, *Socialist Iraq: A Study in Iraqi Politics Since 1968.* Washington, The Middle East Institute, 1978.

Lenczowski, George, "The Arc of Crisis: Its Central Sector." *Foreign Affairs,* Spring 1979.

Long, David E., *The Persian Gulf: An Introduction to Its Peoples, Politics, and Economics,* rev. ed. Boulder, Colorado, Westview Press, 1978.

Nakhleh, Emile, *Arab-American Relations in the Persian Gulf.* Washington, American Enterprise Institute for Public Policy Research, 1975.

Ramazani, R. K., "Security in the Persian Gulf." *Foreign Affairs,* Spring 1979.

Yodfat, A. and Abir, M., *In the Direction of the Persian Gulf: The Soviet Union and the Persian Gulf.* London, Frank Cass, 1977.